On Earth, As It Is In Water

Jordon L. Stanley

ISBN 978-1-62806-361-5 (print | paperback)

Library of Congress Control Number 2022919083

Published by Salt Water Media
29 Broad Street, Suite 104
Berlin, MD 21811
www.saltwatermedia.com

Salt-Water
MEDIA

Cover photo was taken by Gillian Dwyer in Australia 2021
and is used with permission.

For you, for me,
for all that we learned, and endured in 2020.

Contents

On Earth,
As It Is In Water

1

TREE

It wasn't until a conversation about beepers and whether or not I'm old enough to remember them at a family dinner that I realized where I am exactly.

We ate from styrofoam carry out trays that Sunday at grandma Gloria's house and by we I mean the seven of us, out of the usual seven times that.

All had the Corona virus to blame for the TV not being on
showing the game, any game, or the news because we already knew it all.

We all had our cell phones to blame for my uncle giving us a humorous hard time about our heads being down as if the question of who's going to blessed the food wasn't already answered by everyone saying their own grace but I was waiting for the notification to tune into my friends live gender reveal.

And that is where I am exactly. Again.

Thinking about how old I am. How I lost count after 27

When the friends I grew up with. Learned songs with. Memorized scripture, and times tables with.

Played tent revivals with sprained ankles and went on band trips with are having gender reveals for lives that will soon do the same.

I am old enough to remember beepers and two-ways
chorded land lines and that awful song that dial up sang

But at what age are we old enough to know the meaning of life?

Is it the day you're scrolling through Facebook and see a photo of a classmate and someone you didn't even know they knew, with a caption reading "rest in peace, friend"?

Or maybe it's the day you realized that grandma isn't getting around as swiftly as she use to
and you should probably start putting in dibs for some of these books she has sitting on the coffee table. Or her Nintendo Wii, still in the box.

I lost count after 27 but I am reminded anytime someone over 30 tells me I'm young. and that is where I am exactly.

Somewhere between 30 and young carrying the bare minimum about the meaning of life.

Somewhere between 30 and young not knowing what to expect from day to day, writing a poem about not knowing what to expect from day today.

Somewhere between 30 and young, filtering,

Hearing, and believing.

Seeing and receiving.

Shooting the breeze with contentment while calling catastrophe a cab

Seeing trees every day and striving to be like them.

Rooted, grounded.

Responding to the weight of the rain by just letting the water fall, as if this is nothing new.

As if the sadness that rain brings never overrides its nutrients

The next day I get a call from my dad asking for help with moving my grandfathers things out of his barbershop.

The first thing he gives me when I get there is a book.

"Cuttin' Up. Wit & Wisdom From Black Barbershops" by Craig Marberry

and that is where I am exactly.

Loosing count after 27 but counting all 50 plus years of wit and wisdom

years of cuttin' up,

years of being told to hold your head still

Years of heated arguments over the game, any game, or the news.

Years of people coming in already knowing it all.

50 plus years of consistent black owned business behind his helpless eyes.

A friend of mine told me you could either look at the fact that the doors are closing, or the fact that he had them open for as long as he did.

and that is loosing count after 27.

Coming out of, moving on from, anything, more like a tree.

Rooted and grounded.

Responding to the weight of life's rain

By just letting the water fall.

UBIQUITY

(For Roy Ayers)

Feel what I feel when I feel it.

The crunch of the grape,
the chirp of the birds,
the warmth of the sunshine everybody loves.

Do what I do, when I do it

The looseness of the jam,
this avant-garde life.
Even on sad days theres a song.
The melancholic melody,
when the grey in the sky takes a solo,
the blue lays back.
We're all listening to what the clouds have to say.

My life, my life, my life.

When the difference between singing in the rain
and singing in the shower becomes a whisper,
or a wrong note,
the song must continue.
The sourness you taste is a test of your listening pallet.

Folks get down with bees and things.
Folks get brown
flowers.
Brown folks get flowers.
Get honey, reap sunshine.
Everybody loves.
Deep down.

9TH & WE

It was the rain that compelled me to crack you open.

Not like a nut, or a can, or lightning in the sky.

But as a book, hard back.

The scent of your pages become comfort in the chaos.

Change comes, builds momentum, becomes momentary,

leaves creases,

but your words still remain legible.

Your first impression be your headline, your duck and cover.

Hiding place.

Shelter from this rain.

Your contents be the road map,

I maneuver with you.

I know what you consist of.

The footprints in sand

You are footnotes, a guiding hand.

Cross the street with me.

The other side is ours.

It belongs to us.

Here on the corner of 9th and we.

We.

Sharing an umbrella are the only things dry.

The delayed sound of water smiting everything.

Saturating as it does.

All is one constant splash.

On earth, as it is as Adam's Ale.

We say give us this day.

Where options become too heavy to weigh and opinions trespass against us.

Give us the day.

Where person, place, or thing can be too good to be true.

Come what may.

To be abiding is to be as a book.

Preferably closed to possible creases, crisp.

There may even be a crack when you open but your words still remain legible.

ON A BEAUTIFUL DAY

The breeze and the rays from the sun are speaking their best.
One a beautiful day
Theres a couple feeding pieces of bread to the birds at the park.
One a beautiful day,
there is a good book serving you inspiration on a silver plater in the form of its
pages just the same.
One a beautiful day
there is a friend listening to another friends relationship problems, or lack there of.
On a beautiful day
Another friend joins and everyone is just happy to be alive.
On a beautiful day
There's a stranger letting you know that he drank just as much coffee as you be-
cause he keeps walking out of the bathroom at the same time you're walking in.
On a beautiful day
there is a woman carrying peppermint in her purse,
offers you some in hopes that it keeps the flies away.
It doesn't.
But the day remains.
On a beautiful day
Everything says stop and stare at me
and everything is worth it.
and everything is grateful for your time.
On a beautiful day
Everyone with two wheels is riding them.
Everyone with two feet are using them
and everything with 4 wheels has all 4 windows down
On a beautiful day
everything is motivation.
The plant says
"growth takes time and everyone sees it better from their point of view."
The flag says
"you dance your best when the world is blowing around you."
On a beautiful day
there are kids playing on a portable basketball hoop.

Playing on it,

with no basketball.

Picking it up and putting it down having just as much fun as an intense

game of 3 on 3.

If it had been me and my mother was around she would tell us to stop before

we hurt ourselves.

On a beautiful day

the peppermint starts to kick in,

there are things to do that we want to do,

but just not right now.

Our only obligation is this beautiful day.

A FRONT ROW SEAT

Progression is appealing.
To say:
"no that's not where I am anymore"

and be ok with that.

To hear the pouring rain outside clapping on the roof
and say:
"Listen at that water applauding me,
enjoying the show it paid to see."

PEOPLE WATCHING

Have you ever people watched
and in your scan for the most interesting human being you come across that
man in his mid seventies walking around with his head up and hands behind
his back?
Wearing both pleasure and curiosity on his face at the same time?
Amused by everything and nothing?
Looking for the flaw in life as if he lived his without the mention of the
word?

I bet he was there when his grand kids were born.
He probably sat in the waiting room twiddling his retired thumbs because
he was too excited to read a magazine.
I'm sure he has a wife somewhere close by.
At the nail shop.
Having brunch with her sister.
It's a by weekly thing so him and his happy thoughts are happily excused.

He read the paper this morning.
Already had his coffee, no sugar, maybe a little cream.
Don't mind him he just stretching his legs.
One foot in front of the other, heel touching the ground first.
Traveling at the speed of his own ability to read a sign in the window,
or acknowledge a squirrels ability to climb up a tree faster than that.

A polite man,
not only does he smile at the children in the driver seats of the strollers as
their mothers push them by.
He's also considerate of the joggers and bikers
so he stays safely to the right among the slower moving traffic on the street.

I bet he's never gotten into a car accident.
I bet he rarely drives at night.
I bet he's watched NASCAR once.
But will probably go home and watch tennis tonight,

Or golf.

Or maybe he's going home to listen to a record.
I bet he's got a 5 star vinyl collection

I bet he's got more stories than a war vet,
or an imagination that'll make Steven Spielberg take off his hat and scratch his head.

I bet he's seen every western movie known to man.
But likes Sci-fi too.
He probably in a chess club.
Never read a Harry Potter book.

I've probably gone too far.
But I bet you he uses his cell phone with two hands,
peeps a the screen from underneath his glasses,
and would still have a flip phone if FaceTime never became a thing.
Have you ever people watched
and in your scan for the most interesting human being you come across your future self?

TRAIN RIDE

It's hard to ignore
the world whizzing by so fast.
Even with a book.

RECESS

In the spirit of Vince, Spinelli, Gretchen, T.J., Mikey'n 'em.
I aspire to be child like,
but not childish
on the count of imagination knowing no age.

In a perfect world
they'd let us bring a classroom desk
outside for recess.

then we'd have more drummers,
dancers, and producers.
Dreamers, hearers and believers.
Things we can never have enough of.

In this world, though.
When a child screams on a seesaw
delight overwrites.

The thought of a playground
of potential politicians playing fair
is farfetched.

A flock of younglings
all one with the force,
that force being freedom,
so thick you can reach out and flick it,

or bop it, spin it,
pull it, pass it.
Freedom so thick it'll warp
the cuffs off your brain with colors
and numbers but you won't feel a thing.

Just swaying side to side,

tapping your foot.
Blissfully unaware of the change
happening in you.
That's textbook Disney aphorism.
Hold the mirror in front of the world,
replace our reflections with song and dance,

makes it hurt less.
But pain is necessary.
At recess I hurt myself the least
but explored the most.

Something about that fresh air
made even our teachers
let their hair down

but we still looked up to them.
It's up to them.
To do

and be

anything,

and anybody

they want

all in thirty mins.

LATELY

I plan my moments of silence, lately.
Not as promptly as dinner time
But more like "I haven't called my mother in a while.
I should call her at some point today."

Rearranging a room is about a coins flip away from becoming an olympic sport,
lately.
Not quite like heads or tails,
but more like shock put or long jump.
Less like rock paper scissors, more like paper mâché
Anything is what you make it.
As much like paper mâché as pottery, as poetry.

Cellular devices are more of a distraction than normal, lately.
Not quite as much as shoofly fly don't bother me.
Significantly more than shoofly fly don't bother me.
It may actually be better if my phone had wings.

THAT'S IT, THAT'S THE POEM

"My life is a breaker.
Often off
or tripped."

     - Brandon Bartlett

THE MENU

I age half a decade.
I can feel the gray growing.
No one told me that patience is best served hot.
Steamed, foamed, and frothed.
Best served with whatever flavor fills the holes in your boat.
Whatever size fits all you imagine it to be and beyond
you just have to choose it.

No pressure though.
Unless there's someone in line behind you.
The one in front of you is off the hook,
a small fish thrown back,
They've submitted their final answer.
The subdivision, unsurety,
surely theres no take-backsies.

This is America where the options are endless
but the hours you get to weigh them all aren't.
I'm sorry sir, ma'm, you only get 24 here.

These are the days that come and go in a blink
unless you're waiting.
In that case these are the days of the slow and steady.
A sloth slurping a smoothie,
thick,
as thieves, stealing the watch right off your wrist.

These are the days of the "no you're good take your time."
Discuss it with your peers.
Ask them what they're getting.
Just get what they're getting.
Unless they had indecisive for breakfast this morning like you,
then it's back to me.

As the jeopardy theme crescendos from a far
I can see their eyes playing pin ball with the words on the menu.
Or are the words on the menu playing pin ball with their eyes.
Either way.
Would you just light up already?

This coffee shops an arcade.
The jeopardy theme is at full volume,
we're all tapping our feet and swaying side to side
I begin to feel bad for you.

It's overwhelming isn't it?
It all sounds so good doesn't it?
No one really gets one of everything on the menu
do they?

Consider your greed.

Would it help if I showed you a photo?
Just holler and I can answer any questions you may have.
Yes, even the ones with the answer right in front of you.
My mother use to say if it was a snake it would've bit you.
Good thing common sense doesn't have venomous teeth.
Or does it?

EPIPHANY 2/1/21

i

There's magic in relocating.
Maneuvering through life with a new found super power is the real journey.
This must be what Peter Parker felt the morning after the bite.
Suddenly, there's inner increase where there was none.
Suddenly, you've placed two feet on the welcome mat at 30's house,
and as she looks at you through the peep hole you realize
that the best things in life really are free,
and things that cost a buck become fluff.
Your definition of what it means to arrive rearranges.
What once fueled a desire to have, or to be, dwindles.
And balance, or lack there of becomes uncomfortable.
What is awareness to the lost and never found?
It is to think you're behind the wheel but in reality you are the wheel.
Merely an instrument.
Don't you want to be the music?

ii

Which is better?
The song of freedom or the caged bird that sings it?
Wondering how long the whistling wind can hold a whole note,
never running out of breath until it wants to.
Which is better?
The musician playing to heal self
keeping his own head above water?
Or playing to heal the earth, becoming the water?
Becoming the 71 percent.
Suddenly, you're the majority.
The minority has just been crying wolf,
swimming in their own kiddy pool of tears,
when you have been Angel Falls your whole life,
and just had an epiphany today.
What will you do with that?

IRISH GOODBYE

It's amazing how space works.
That middle ground between introvert and extrovert
is the couch I sleep on when I crash at a friends house.
Pros of being an ambivert.
You're never on either end of the social spectrum
long enough to unpack and make yourself at home.
But home is that 10-14 days between social butterfly
and lone cocoon.
At no point does the butterfly ever feel lost.
Just unsettled.
Just a passer-by, passing through.

I am Sherlock Holmes with a compass for a heart.
I am Jack Black with Aretha Franklin's stamp of approval.
Teaching kids how to Rock Steady in their schools,
but can't tell you the last time
I've been able to call this song exactly what it is.
Cant' tell you the last time I've felt certain
in that domicile.
Can't tell you the last time I've played *I spy* on a road trip,
or punch someone,
and deem it illegal to punch me back when I saw a punch buggy first.

Wherever I go I am not home.
Wherever I grow,
it is blasphemy to ask me to take my shoes off when I get there.
I am not staying.
My guts and glory are already at my next stop.
I am prepped and primed to feel disquiet when I get there.

So forgive me if I sometimes just get up and go.
I put the *i* in Irish Goodbye.
One could say that I'm addicted to my freedom.

It's the last thing I scroll through at night,
it is the first thing I check in the morning.
I hold it so tight it sometimes makes indents in my chest,
I vowed to never lose it again.

A movers mantra seldom welcomes hospitality.
But they're on a constant search for pieces of home.
Whatever and wherever that may be.

AN OPEN LETTER TO MILES MORALES, THE BLACK SPIDER-MAN

What's it like being able to drink your coffee upside down?
I imagine you like your coffee like you.
Strong and black.
It must be sweet to be bilingual and bad ass.
Wanted dead or alive by grown men,
Meddling and married to their madness.

You be just a kid, younger than your predecessor.
Smaller than your enemies.
Anything Pete can do, you can do better.
I've seen it.
Yet we've seen nothing like you.

You save Brooklyn and rep Brooklyn simultaneously.
Timberlands laced loosely,
Hood up, backpack strapped.
A safe place for your iPhone, head phones, bus pass, wallet.
A savior and safe house.
A soft place for the neighborhood cat.

Us regular smegular, damsels in distress down here
we struggle to walk and chew gum in sync but, you.
You beat box the Grindin' beat by Clipse as you zip
from ghetto to ghetto, to back yard, to yard,
from building, to ceiling, to wall.
Alright by Kendrick Lamar be your sound track as you swing
as you super.
As you hero.

I'm sorry the world hasn't experienced you sooner,
but you couldn't have come at a better time such as this.
A T'Challa and George Floyd simultaneous salute.
Picking up the baton Static Shock dropped while it was still smoking.

It could very well be that the pressure of that universe
was too much for him but here,
in this one,
You know the vibe.
And I can only imagine what it's like.
To be the new Spiderman.
"This ones cooler.
Cooler looking."
More powers.
More mystery, more myth.
Maybe even a higher pain tolerance.
I don't know.
But I do know what it's like to feel overwhelmed.
To have your mother call while you're juggling seven things at once,
phone in one hand, bad guy in the other, bullets flying, and sirens howling
At the sun, at the moon.

With great power comes greater equanimity.

I know what it's like to wish everyday for the screeching halt that you'll never hear.
When they just won't let you have a moment.
A day.
The needs they know no wait, they only know now.
The requests, the constant cries for help they know no slumber.
As do you.

New York's friendly neighborhood drum major.
Marching to the beat of the hero's burden.

At all times be sure to bounce.
Bounce to brass and bass.

Down here we clap for you.
We clap for you with helpless hands,
we cheer you on with clanging cymbals.

Praise!

In awe of your eco friendliness,
In awe of how perfectly you are cardboard cut out for this.
Even on your worst day.

WE GLOW

For we are His workmanship
and O, how good it is.
O, how good it is to know exactly what to do
with all these lemons life keeps handing us.

To look at rubble and ruin
and see more than rubble and ruin
To see hurt,
trumped by hope
and a burning belief that life is more
than what happen to you.

That happiness is based on happenings
but that is nothing in comparison to
inner light and the power of
get back up.

Of course a single day of dark
transcends into a lifetime when we
underestimate the power of a simple hug.

Of course we will walk around defeated
when no one around us is using their smile.
Of course some days will be better than others
but each day keeps happening.
Each day is a chance to chip away
at ourselves.

The most beautiful thing I've ever seen
is the perfect display of emotional awareness
and strength.

The best stories are of people who've
looked defeat in the face

and said *swerve.*

The most annoying thing on this earth
are complainers
who ride shotgun,

strapped in stagnancies seat belt
searching for a sign
they wont be able to see.

Lighting the world is growing.
Lighting the world is learning.
Lighting the world is loving.

We are carpenters and we are the tools

Building is doing.
Building is believing.
Building is loving.
and our work here isn't done until its done.

2

RESPOND

When things are moving.
When the things around you are making music
are you listening?

Do you let yourself dance to it?
Or does the key bother you?
What about the tempo?
Too fast?
Too slow?
Do you observe first?
Watch other peoples steps
try to memorize the moves before you jump in?
Or are you okay in the corner dancing by yourself?

For the past few weeks
I've had the sudden urge to go dancing
and find the music myself when there is none.
I'm impatient in that way.
Because silence is also essential.
How does one wait for the music and enjoy the silence trusting that the music will
come?
It always does.
I guess what really matters is how we respond.

THE MOST BEAUTIFUL THING WE'VE NEVER SEEN

No one ever really cares about the in-between.
The end and the beginning are aways more fun to write home about.
I feel for the in-between,
the same way that I feel for the emotionally strong, and the mentally ripped.

No one really cares about the in-between.
How much time things that take time really take.
I care about what you learn while you wait.
What you've learned there.
There being everything and nothing.
Everywhere and home.
There being rest and restlessness
but that doesn't mean it matters less.
Doesn't make it any less real.
The in-between is substance and sustenance
Necessity, and now.
It is tasteful, rich.
Void of fame, absent of director and script.

I care about the in-between.
a man, human.
In the in-between himself.
Questioning the end, having reflected on the beginning.
That being an occasional rewind, it is breakfast in bed.
It is the movie, but never dinner.
The in-between,
that being a full course meal of self.
The bite off of more than you can chew.
An excellent source of fiber for the readers digest.
I digress.

The end,

untouched, unhooked.

The most beautiful thing we've never seen

impossible to regret, yet.

For it we are always or never prepared?

Thanks be to the in-between.

WHAT IT MEANS...

i

These days it is 4am when I am the most awake.
I sit, staring out of a floor to ceiling window admiring the impossible from a
D.C. sky.
Watching snow fall after a 60 degree day in early Januray.
I think of change.
How it is to be human to change
and refuse to.
How even the sky can up and decide that it wants to see a blanket of white
over everything when just yesterday we gave even our lightest of jackets the
side eye.
And we just adjust.

I think of how what I want out of life has changed.
My priorities.
Where I am, what I choose to do.
And I think of all the humans that adjust
and refuse to.
To see my change as catastrophe.
The selfishness one must be swimming in.
When human sees humanness as piranha and not Nemo.
I want to ask them what they believe in.
Beg their pardon,
point to the ground, or the sea.
Point to a forest, ignoring a single tree.

ii

Somewhere in the middle of it's gratitude,
art pities us for our inability to see the bigger picture.
Admitting when something is beyond you is a simple brush stroke.
Stillness is framing a snapshot of the hurtles you've jumped.
The discipline you've dug up out of the soil of your many spars with sufferance.

Sing! The songs of the sound mind.
Say: Survival of the stoic.

...TO BE HUMAN

When there's nothing to say of substance
Silence is the cat scratching at the door.
The sun and the moon become the only thing to marvel over.
I enjoy them more than I enjoy most people.
Life then becomes more abstract art than it's ever been and the sky becomes
less of the limit, less the merrier more a mirror.
To be human is to look at a single crumb on a table and identify with it.
To be human is to imagine anything.
Say: *I am to be marveled over.*
I, whole, mortal.
Freely fickle, can be anything at any given moment.
Yet still unquestionably human.
It is my privilege and my pleasure.

THE RACE THING

What's that thing called?
Who gave it to you?
Do you mock it because of its vanguard benefits?
Did you take one down and pass it around
like bread at a table of your ancestors and relatives?
How much did it cost?
And are you still paying for it?
What's your monthly? Freedom or oppression?
Traditional? Or open to suggestions on something a little more fresh,
individual, or new?
Do people even care?
How often are you heard?
I mean really heard.
Whether within or out of your tribe.
The popular population where you reside,
sharing inherited physically and biological traits.
It's Race.

RECYCLE

Always consider
the box people put you in.
Saving the planet.

FORGETTING SOMETHING

For so long we've moved for a living.
Theres been no gravity on our stillness.
Our thoughts and ideas bounce and float so far from home,
no concept of time.

The hands on our clocks always pointing to the next thing.
Leaving another behind.
Late because we've back tracked.
Naughty because we didn't make a list and check twice.

It's always time to go.

Always a time to straighten up and fly right.
Never time to perch and observe,
to perch and process before proceeding.
Assuming is for the birds.

Though I'm ground bound I shall not move loud.
How profound that rationality and rest
are the keys to moving in silence.

What have you gained from the *grab'n go?*
Imagine Wilma Rudolph ignoring the mark and the get set
Imagine only the mark and the get set.
Their importance in comparison to the go.

Why being where you are has a cardinal effect on the journey to.
Why COVID 19 changed the pace of this red light green light game of life.
To call red and then leave
only to come back months later to call yellow and then leave again.

So addicted to the go that you don't know
what you're running from you're actually running with.
It is to be human to be shaped by circumstance,

after all we have five senses so it is human to be sensitive.

To wonder if your variations of being are enough.
To see greener grass over there.
To be home and know that there is no place like it.

It is human to be alone while in the company.
To be torn between staying
or going.

A color can not determine the who, what, where, and why
my worry has always been the when.
And when I see that green light,
I just hope I'm not forgetting something.

ATTRACTING OPPOSITES

#StayHome has me asking question like,
"I wonder how much more fun of a game whack a mole would be
if they gave you a pistol instead of a mallet with a cushion on the end?"

Your aggression is your defense.
My peace is my pistol.
I've never seen thoughts do that.

You assume and respond.
I analyze, carry the 2, and show my work.

You think out loud to tune out the voices inside.
I listen closely, find the rhythm in their words and write to it.

Silence to you
Smells like question marks and past pain.
You seek change.
Yet change finds me.
Dead president heads on copper and silver
constantly clanging, making music in my pocket.
I'm writing to that too.

You cut your hair to fight the feeling.
I grow my hair to feel the fight.
The rebel in me won that battle a long time ago,
but the war..

Your aggression is your defense.
My peace is my pistol.
I've never seen thoughts do that.
They move like Moles but all I have is this mallet
with a cushion on the end.

A NOTEWORTHY WEEKEND IN 2020

Starts alone and ends alone as most of them do.
Most of them do subject themselves to lonelinesses personal chauffeur on piggy back.
How many times has a phone call at 1 am not end in a story to be told in years to come?
It's amazing what a flat tire can do.
It's amazing what time can tell.
How even with the loss of a father a brotherhood can never miss a beat.
The heart of a drummer always knows where 1 is, though 2 and 4 may sometimes get away from him.

Every funeral that summer was one long game of Guess Who?
We trained our minds to recognize people by their walks.
It took us forever to be fluent in the language of suffocate.
Oh, the irony of a face mask reading "I cant breathe" hitting you in the face.
The humor of people being exactly who they are will always top charts.
The joy of sharing community joy is a race thing, should never not be an annual thing.
How many shares did you get on that, about two? Five? How many hearts did you get when you went live?
How many times did I hear the words "live stream"?
How many deep breaths you take without a mask? Away from people, outside of yourself. About as many moments as you relished just because they were good.
Just because no one was asking you a question, or selling you something, or advertising everything but what you actually needed.
Requesting, requiring. Its' tiring.
But space becomes rejuvenating, and
people are putting the word *hopeful* in colorful colors, on signs, on flags, on bumper stickers, hiding its meaning in their hearts.
I read the back of the book and we win.
But what is a victory when you're waring against no one?

It is gifting ice to an eskimo.

It is giving keys to the driver but not telling them where the car is.

It is a safe return home after a high speed car chase whizzes by you.

It is the hazel eyed, gemini, passenger, with an appetite for adventure sleeping through that. Eventful, noteworthy.

Character traits for the qualified of your time.

Awareness, discernment.

Character traits for the qualified to survive.

WORKING FROM HOME

The sound of summer I've been looking for.
Kids next door
screaming bloody murder in a pool of water.
With pure 90 degree joy
and all of Maryland's humidity holding the knife.

THANKSGIVING 2020

It's two o'clock in the afternoon and I am YouTubing how to use the espresso machine in the kitchen. The sound of running water pouring from the faucet is competing with the irony in the room as a young Michael Jackson and his four brothers sing a song from the Alexa about how Christmas won't be the same this year. But it's thanksgiving and there's a lot to be thankful for.

For every sip I take, my aunt slides a task across the counter. A bowl of boiled eggs to be deviled. Potatoes to be mashed. Vegetables to be diced. There are sounds but I could dice the silence in the room with the same knife. I heard the pin drop of the past. How last year, this time, I am doing victory dances in the front yard with a hangover. Our usual attendance, somewhere around fifty or sixty. A portion of that, split up into two teams, identified by red and yellow velcro flags, this is an annual competitive brawl for us. That year it was freezing. But we had ourselves to keep us warm. Today it is 65 degrees.

It's five o'clock in the evening, dinner was supposed to be an hour ago, and this is the first time I've ever seen my mother hangry. She sits to the table with her head in her hand. The remaining four of us trickle into a table that seats eight, I'd say the table was about half full. None of us finished our plates. We nibbled so much while cooking that we barely ate anything when dinner was done. Just more to take home. It was at home eating leftovers that I heard the pin drop of therapist again. Last year, this time, I didn't finish my plate either. I sat next to a cousin, the only available seat at one of the eleven tables, by the TV with the game on. Hunched over, shuffling mac and cheese around some stuffing with my fork. Exchanging about grandma Lou and how this is the first dinner without her. How her funeral was the last time I saw him. In and out of small talk that didn't really bother me because it was thanksgiving and there is a lot to be thankful for.

TAKE ME THERE

I remember it.
Missing what it felt like to go.
Feeling stillness breathe down your neck.
Ignorance laughing in the other room.
How hard it was then, to not be able to hear
past your own eager.
To exhaust your own welcome in your own home.

Take me there.
I can handle it.
Audacity at its all time low.
Considering another meant considering self.
People were people,
things were things.
Whether moving or stagnant.
People as polar opposites,
expressing their similarities.
Hitting ignore when their differences call.
Or is this the arrival?
Is this phoning a friend?
That friend being home,
that home being the genesis
or the revelations.
A destination we can be proud of.

WHEN YOU ASK A BLACK MAN ABOUT LONELINESS...

his first instinct is to give you the watered down version.
Scenarios you'd find on Disney+.
The ones with obvious creases,
you can predict how it unfolds.
There may even be a song you like.
One you've memorized the lyrics to,
your kids can sing it in their sleep.

When you ask a black man about loneliness,
and he trusts you,
this is not your first R rated movie.
You have the stomach for blood and guts.
You ain't covering your eyes and ears,
you may even have a potty mouth yourself.
You may even have a considerable amount of awareness
 of the backwards bend.

How sometimes it feels like your spine ain't even there.
But the one thing always there, is the one thing a surgery can't change
and a change of the mind is the one thing a surgery cant nip or tuck.

So ask a black man about loneliness
and in all thy asking, ask for understanding
in whatever version he gives you.

Whether it leaves you in disbelief or
disgust make sure you chew that food well.
What you're tasting is an every day flavor for some of us.
The same way that hate is an everyday flavor for people
that can't even handle it themselves.

I once watched a man spit 16 times out of the window of his truck,

once on every letter of the Black Lives Matter street painting.
Or maybe it's not a mattering matter.

It's the bare minimal, but maybe its visual.
On a gig once, for 3 hours I watched people put money in a tip jar,
make eye contact and say thank you
to everyone in the band accept me.

Ask a black man about loneliness
and he may even tell you about not being black enough
because his vernacular is too white.
Once upon a time,
if they wanted to hide something from us
they'd put it in a book.

Why live my life waiting for dropped gems so I can recycle
and claim to drop a mic,
when all I have to do is go find them and I can keep them for myself?
That was the objective of every good game right?

Spyro, Crash Bandicoot, Zelda.
See, acknowledged, collect, defeat.
Sounds familiar, right?
Nowadays it's just upgrade and cheat.
Sounds familiar, right?
Be one up, the next man down,
look around,
see everyone and no one concomitantly.
See everyone in small town,
know your story,
but wont care enough to not bend the pages
when they read the book.

Ask a black man about loneliness
and he'll tell you how his joy
isn't the same as yours.

He'll agree that it should be.
But it's one thing to have your day ruined
by a video of someone killed innocently.

It's another when in all the videos
the person killed looks like you.
And you try.

You try to hose down your assumptions
because you know
if you let that prejudice flam kindle,
It'll keep you warm at night.

Tis the season to be chilly right now.
Everybody is chilly when the sun goes down,
right now.
And everybody gets lonely too.

A PROUD BLUES FOR HUGHES

I went to bed listening to Langston last night.
Woke up proud of the blackness in my berry.
Having rid myself of all the bitter in my juice.
It's sweet how amazing grace is.

I use to wonder what sound taste like.
And marvel at the expanding pallet of man.
How what is now music to your ears,
you once turned your nose up to.

I marvel at the distance between here and there.
How every pair of shoes made
aren't actually supposed to be traveled in.
Yet, every weight you carry is a bag that has to be checked.

Today I am headed for the boarder,
borderline light as a feather.
One right move, and one good wind gust might
make Lenny Kravitz proud
and Jordan join the league a 3rd time.
One small step for man,
one giant leap for the blackness in man,
kind of proud, kind of loud,
maybe that's what sound tastes like.

Taste like going to bed listening to Langston only to dream like King.
Wake up at the crack of dawn aspiring to inspire like Boseman or Cicely.
If you fought like Tyson you'd have a record like Ali too.

These names were our first escape.
An early introduction of hope from people that look like us.
They kept in our peripheral

the difference between living and dying.

As you click, as you scroll,
as you buy and sell,
as you go and as you come,
you ever think to yourself
what am I doing here?

Then tip your hat to those who've painted that yellow brick road,
or sewed that red carpet, or polished that silver spoon,
those who've paved the way,
you wonder if they're the least bit proud of us.

And it is there, as you lick your lips,
as you run your finger through your hair,
as you fall into the current,
you can't decide which is sweeter,
the taste of grace,
or it's subtle hum like the fridge in the kitchen.

You don't know it's there until you hear it
break the silence in the room when
the noise of the world stops for a breather.

When the noise of the world impels you
and governs your thoughts about yourself
it's their voices that push back end redirects them.

Some singing the scent of survival,
and others taming your timidness with a simple touch.
"One thing we gon' always be is here", you hear.

In a voice resembling and even blend of Denzel Washington
and Morgan Freeman,
and maybe that is whats so amazing about grace.
Its propensity to sounds and taste like
freedom, strength, and pride, in the present.

5/26/21

Theres only one thing to do when the power is out
and the sky's stomach is growling.
When the moon and its blood red beauty stole the show last night.
The Blue Angles and their Navy pride stole the show yesterday.

Tonight the clouds are portraying a delayed paparazzi.
Taking snap shots of us from the view up there,
you can see the flash.

Tonight from my balcony,
Instead of watching my neighbors TV
I choose the darkest cloud and ask it how I look.
It will respond *"I don't know how you do it."*
"...Do what?" I ask.
"How you write in the rain."

3

THE MORNING AFTER A DAY OFF

On the days when my life resembles the birds I so envy
the entire world beneath me is left on read.
The seasoning of this season becomes buoyant again.
I'm aware of its flavor.

She could've easily sent a typical good morning text,
but instead she says
"Back To The Grind What Are You Reading?"
Well, I'm in between two things right now,
this book in front of me, and you.

I've been working on my spacial awareness.
Y'all call it social distancing.
I call it knowing where you correctly fit.
And on the days when my life doesn't quite resembles the birds I so envy,
I still resort to the sky because down here, I never really know where that is.
O, the luxury of flying high when the low gets too crowded.
And the last place you settled gets shuffled.
O, the luxury of flying high when good morning isn't so good.
It becomes back to the ground.
It becomes back to the grind.

NOW AND LATER

I can't tell if it's the music it once made
or the music it makes
when I admire
the clock on the wall.
Its tick something of a lullaby.
Resonating a bit longer.
A half second to be exact.
Its black hands make white noise.
Keeping time better than mine ever will.
Now and later
The silence in my home is hard and sweet.
Copper and bronze and coffee call me.
Every hour on the hour
there should be a crash.
An emphasis on the 1.
A subtle record of every moment under it.
I envy its rational.
How round its routine is.
It is what I aspire to be.
An instrument.
Consistent.
High sitting, all seeing,
but only heard when listened to.
Only speaking when spoken to.
Moving to music while still.
Satisfied in silence or just plain present.
A gift and a keeper
of now and of later.

ONE DAY AT A TIME

The older I get the more I redefine things.
Mornings, nights.
Moments, thoughts, sounds, peace.
Particularly patience.
I wait better now.
This race be slow and steady.
These trophies,
these medals and plaques prove that.
Prove that proving nothing to you
is proving all things slow and steady to me.
Security be
less social
more solid as a rock.
Heavy as a day.
Light as time.

How do we define what is divine?
Meeting a follower?
Running into a friend?
These things happen when we let go.
When we let *going* loosen its grip on us
we become closer to the magic within.
The magic around us be just that.
How else can a big world feel back pack
yet full of so many things that touch our hearts
when we let them?
Let them.

Let them not know.
Even you.
Choose to not know
and watch the runway grow out of the ground beneath you.
Be unsure for a second and watch your back pack turn jet pack.
Flying is living.

Living is loose.
One day at a time.

WHEN 30 KNOCKS

With great power comes
great responsibility:
An early bed time.

FOUR WISHES FOR YOU

What does it mean when your thoughts of someone are as high as the sky?
How do you measure their value when they are more than the angel in their throat?
Summoning Gabriel at the hum of their favorite hymn.
Living life psalm by psalm,
poem by poem,
work by work.
Colorful be the journey of a doer,
and I wish your journey bowls of Chop't.
And I wish your mind the nutrition it needs.
Healthy be your thoughts of yourself.
Concrete be your confidence.

I can imagine how proud your parents are of you.
To have birthed someone with ambitions that roar like a lion
yet their countenance is that of a butterfly,
reminding us all of how good transformation can be for the body.
To go halfsies on a human with a smile that slices through doubt like a knife through butter.
I wish for you that time takes it's time.
I wish for you that the earth returns to you what you've rendered it.
That every honest answer to questions like "how are you?"
becomes wind in your sail and there be no humidity where you touch down,
but space and opportunity to feel what you feel, and be, and see, and observe.
Gather, collect, process, progress.
You will see your gain,
Avert regret.
The world awaits your next season.
Amen.

LOUD SEGMENTS OF RANDOM CONVERSATION BETWEEN THREE TABLES

"I am from South Carolina."

"I starved to death for the first couple of meals."

"But I learned to use chop sticks, so thats good"

"Did you finish your exam?"

"Rather unfortunate"

"I can't get my microphone to work!"

"I feel like I should give you some more background."

"I am dying to go there."

"My boyfriend is an absolute softy."

"I think he may have gotten his masters in it."

"Yeah yeah, right right."

"He at one point got married and went on his honey moon in Madagascar."

"Yeah, very strange"

"He is now divorced."

"I don't care what color, I just want BIG"

"I would like to share my gifts with you."

"Her name is Bailey, she is a Golden Lab I believe."

"Everything is an illusion."

"Right, right, right."

"I literally have a quiet time."

"And then theres poetry thats been done before, I guess like more 'poet'…"

"My dad was like 64 at the time."

"I feel a great deal of peace right now."

JORDAN PEELE

A sharp shooter.
The man doesn't miss.
The only mind that I anticipate
to see on screen so much it burns.
I'd bottle that flame if I could.

We snapped out fingers
more than Soulja Boy in 07'
when *Us* came out.
Trying to find the beat,
trying to make it make sense.

Only you can spoon feed me
horror and reality.
Realities taste and texture
like movie theater butter and bubbles
who knew that you could open the world wide and
shove black joy down
its throat?

Like we're not the song
America has been skipping
all its life and just now
found out that its fire.
You watch as America
attempts to bottle that,
burns itself
snaps to a beat that isn't there,
listen, then grant us the
answered prayer that is *Nope*
for that we say yes
to you.

That gun holster full of film

doesn't end does it?
Is it Sunken Place deep?

The surface Hollywood
thought it was scratching
until you showed up.
Feeling what we feel
saying what we been saying
showing us what we've
been wanting to see like the good griot
you are, with ease.

We toast in appreciation
imaginations like yours.
Handing us back the authority
over the things we fear
like change in exchange for the nightmares
that had us by our throats,
for the balls to tell the stories
that had us by them.

Wedge by wedge of the journey
they are blind to.
Once is not enough.
Calling them easter eggs is an
understatement, and offensive.
I call them layers of brilliant bijou.

You live in between the lines
yet can see the floor of our emotions
like a point guard
giving us stories that don't drag.
Strategic as a game of chess.
I reached for my seatbelt instead of
the recliner button the third time I saw Get Out.
Quite possibly the greatest movie

of our time, I can't exaggerate.

But I can support.
Flawless foreshadowing.
The visual poetry that is art
imitating the rawness of life.
Optically groundbreaking, gratifying.

A remnant of mankind is indebted to you.
Determination of this demeanor
demands dinner discussion.

Barbershop talk should evolve
from who dunked on who,
and who's getting paid to trade to:
what on earth will you do next?

We will know
when thunder resounds in broad daylight,
when rainbows appear at random,
when our doppelgänger's wear
red jump suits and join hands across the country,
when money and keys rain from
clouds that haven't moved in days.
We will know
what on earth you will do next
when you're ready for us to.

UNSTOPPABLE

Downtown Silver Spring,
I saw a black boy skateboarding in Timberlands
And he was actually landing tricks.
A birth right.
Unmoved by defeat.
As if to say:
"I don't hear can't
Only *Can* and *Will, On God,*
and *How Much You Wanna Bet?*"

Surrounded by peers but in your own world still.
As if their world was lava, or contagious.
And yours a throne.
Tell me what it means to be unstoppable
without telling me what it means to be unstoppable.
The end to your reign ain't around the mountain
coming when she comes.
The end of your reign ain't existed since you laced those boots
and landed that kick flip.
And finish a Fakie Bigspin with flawless recovery.
Yeah bro, I saw it.
Kareem Campbell would be proud.

SUBSCRIBING TO RESILIENCE

I often love when a song doesn't end the way it starts
That groove hits different when listening is a journey,
such as life.
That melody hits different when you felt yourself lift out of your seat a little bit.

Why on earth should I be okay with returning back to the beginning?
Why on earth should the departure from earth
end with returning back?

I believe that if the exhausted end to a stretch is to break,
then we should be okay with the unexpected end.
We should be okay with movement in an unknown direction
and okay with the desire to never see what once was again.

I understand that bad is subjective
I prefer to *break from* or a *break from*
as opposed to the *break in*.

I subscribe to resilience
but I am married to the move.
We can't decide if our anniversary is the day I took my first steps
or made my first bit of progress,
either way,
I am loyal to the move, and she is loyal to me.

But I often love when a poem ends the way it starts.
Those words hit different when the journey from heart to mind
from mind to mouth from mouth to ear
hit home like an astroid to earth
and makes you come out of your seat a little bit.

I believe that if a fresh beginning to comfort is attachment

then we should pray to never fall in love with the music home makes,
and we should often love songs that don't end the way they begin.

For some, listening may be the only journey,
And subscribing to resilience may be the only stretch that won't break you.

CHANGE FOR A $20

Because we missed yesterdays chance to change
Tomorrows $10, $5, and five $1s remains a hope.
This bill recalls its date of birth,
calls the God it claims to trust.

Counts all the seconds and hours it equals to.
I recall all the words ever spoken to me,
the cents they amounted to.
The sense some never made.

The remnants of my life that remain
unchanged since exchanged words.
In some ways I wish it cost to say.

Truth would be cheaper than a lie.
Currency as collateral for finished fruition
An economy excellent.
Excitement perfectly placed.

Imagine trusting and believing
anything.
Imagine trusting and believing,
everything.

That gut feeling of a fib flying from face to face far removed
Intuition on the top shelf collecting dust
next to the red flags, and caution tape.

Wonder wandering in the wind.
Because words would warrant currency.
Honesty, raw and sweet straight from the cane.

Truth.

Time and energy never misplaced
But frank and forthright intentions floating freely.

Chirping like birds in the morning,
Warm as the sun on a spring day.

Yeah, I'd pay to see that too.

THE POETRY EVERYWHERE

She asked me what we should cheers to.
Fiddling with the lime in her glass,
kebabed by a toothpick,
wadding in waters of pink and ice
calling itself The Color Purple.

Suddenly, I am a teacher.
All the things around me are students with one arm vertical,
waving their hands vehemently
as if to say "pick me".

The weary blueberries in my glass,
the paper straw that never stood a chance
dissipating with every nervous stir.

waving

The uninterested teenager wearing one ear pod,
spoon feeding him lyrical nonsense by
a rapper with *Lil* in front of their name;
amongst the happy couple fanning the flame of their love at the table behind me

waving

the fifth car in a row that has pulled a U-turn
in the middle of a street the width of a slim jim

waving

the server who,
wearing a mask and an accent,
couldn't quite throw his name over the plate so that I could catch it

waving

the color scheme on the buildings,
on the walls,
of the people.
With intentions as random as the stars.
Full of depth and definition.
Sparse.

waving

The scent of coming rain.
Vanilla, tobacco, collate.
Perfectly prepared food for the soul lacking nothing of love.

The woman at the table to my left telling the Brotha' sitting across from her
"because I am your mother and I love you."

Loving

The soft rain lasting just long enough to wet the whistle of
the buildings,
and the walls
with intention and definition.

Loving

The paper straw in my glass becoming a soggy slim jim.
Depthless.

Suddenly, I am present again.
And the only thing left to do is raise my glass.

GOLD

*"I use to look at every opportunity I got as either a lesson or reward
but now the older I get I realize it's always both." - Ricky Jefferson*

I dream.
I dream of
The sunny side of everything
The quiet side of the sun
Silent as the S in Arkansas.
Silent as tomorrow, as the scent of a new day.

I dream of the fist bump.
Between will and what will.
Happiness happens whether we want or don't deserve.
Whether we have or hate to hope
to hold what we don't.

Dream.
Like to be awake is to illuminate
what you choose to hide in the dark.
Dream like all comes to light because orbiting is inevitable
Like all comes to light when you submit to the orbit of everything
As if all is not round
As if the fat lady with a choir in her chest wont roll if she trips
saving days light.
dropping days mic.

Whats in a sound?
Vibration dreaming?
Our senses waking up?
Hearing the ding of truth?
It's warmth as a robe
as a touch you wont forget
As an answer correct.

What's in a dream?

Night?
Day?
All?
Nothing?
The solitude in between?
Real reeling us in
reaching for our attention for us?
Pointing out what we choose to ignore in real life?

Dream.
Like all is false.
A red X, a family feud buzzer
An answer incorrect.
All that is real is in and of yourself.
Imagine that.
A walking window of imagination.
Imitation looks in and is intimidated.
In turn, turns and walks away.
Challenged.
By virtue of self.
It is a delicacy to be too good to be true.
Literally not lightly.
It's lit, really.
Reality.
Tangibility.
Touchable things holding value
As self evident truths.
But your ideas.
Your thoughts,
Your energy, your effort.
Your unseen.
Your Dreams.
Gold.

THAT ONE DAY I JUDGED A MAN BY THE COVER OF HIS BOOK

It's always the quiet days where people seem to talk the loudest.
The lobby is a hidden gem, the people that come here know what's up.
We're in agreement, this is merely a pit stop in the pace of our day.
We come in peace, for peace.
We are not to speak unless spoken to,
turn your page, sip your drink, breathe, blink.

A man walks in, haven't seen him yet, just heard him.
Heard his entire drink order
a large mocha.
Smelled him,
his entire series of questions, reeked of small talk, and sweat.
He sits at my eleven o'clock.
the book I'm holding twelve.
his book, a hard back, tucked under his arm,
throws it on the table, removes his mask,
pulls out his phone.
Takes a seat

Minutes have passed,
In my *page turning* I glance at him.
Cellular device in hand.
by the smirk on his face
revealing the chuckle at the ready
he's probably reading a meme,
scrolling through his friends list
adding the names and clicking "share"
I read on.

In my *drink sipping* I glance at him

in hopes that he would get in formation,
turn your page, sip your drink, breathe, blink
minutes have passed
and finally,
his phone face up to the right of him,
two handing his book,
the cover, white with red and black letters,
unable to make out what it reads,
I read on
Breathe, blink.

Minutes have passed
In my *page turning,*
someone else in the room *sips their drink,*
I glance at them,
and watch as our sequence is ceased by our meme slinging, Mr. Mocha, over there
flaring up in laughter with his book face down and his phone in hand.
The legs of a chair scrape the floor as someone with their back towards him turns around,
suddenly aware of his existence.
He never looks up one time.
Never even acknowledging his acknowledgment.
Mr. Mocha never knew where he was.
I shut my book,
sip my drink and imagine what thats like.
I imagine it's like being so use to your own volume at 120db
that you lost sight of proper library etiquette
breathe, blink.
I imagine it's like not being able to put your phone down long enough to read a chapter of a book.
breathe, blink
He just sat there thumbing away the present
while we thumbed our pages in appreciation.
paddling in the puddle of our own peace.
Sip your drink, breathe, blink.

MOMENTS IN THE KEY OF NOW

"whatever it is that keeps me going, is more than me."
- Kentavius Jones

Irony in the key of sound.
Rings like coincidence.
Smells like the present.
Burns like dialogue the night before as oil and wick.
Notes of earth and leather appear when the fire of a city consumes the people of a small town.
You ask yourself,
Do you trap here, or are you trapped here?
As the neighbor next door shows off the sound system in their truck.
The trunk rattles, the hi hats hiss, and spit. Louder the conversation gets in competition with the sound and scent of now.

Mumble rap seems to be everywhere and in everything, you think.
It's comforting though, depending on where you are when you hear it.
It's the book you can't put down,
The thing that keeps you where you should've left 10mins ago.

Next thing you know you're lingering and now
your scene goes black and white.
Now your *now* is wasted in red letters and all caps.

You think of what you missed.
You think of what they miss
when they comment on your patience.

Your outer: a zen Buddhist with legs in crochet.
But your inner: chaotic.
Your nightly laze, that of a war vet.

The power in your composure on the daily
becomes your daily bread.
You clench all things good to you
and good for you closer to you.

You count them.

They are precious.
None of which are your image,
none of which are yourself and you call them good.
Some of which are the things you've learned about those surrounding.
Who you can expect to say what.
What you can expect them to choose over you, or not.

The pedals on a flower amount not to peoples patterns and prints.
You pride yourself on listening.
You read between the lines with your ears.
You hear them coming a mile away because
you aren't too busy asking questions
that you already know the answers to.
Yet, you don't assume because that's what context clues are for.

Even in this *now*, though frustrating still.
The things you can't control may think
they have a hold on you.
But you are as wild as the waves.

You change like the seasons with no one else's permission
but your own.
Wear that ware and tare of the extra mile for everyone else
like your Sundays best,
like it's Justin Timberlake's Suit and Tie,
let me show you a few things.

Show them a few things.
Show them how Type A you are not.

How variety is the spice of life but improv;
Improvisation is the secret ingredient.

Forbearance is the thing in your sauce they can figure out.
What you are here in the key of this very now
matters more than whatever song they want you to get to later on in your set.
Matters more than whatever irrelevant song request
a stranger throws at you with, or without, a twenty dollar bill behind it.

You tell them to get an iPod, or turn on the radio.
You tell them to wake up.
You tell them that originality is the key of *now*,
and knowing it's way too far out of their range.
You sing your song unapologetically, anyway.

WATER
(A Scorpio's theme)

You can count on me to contradict.
You can count on me to go where I don't belong
and do whats not allowed to be done there.
Wear a Coke-A-Cola shirt while guzzling a two liter Pepsi.
Drink wine out of a mason jar.

But this isn't a poem about morality and opposites.

You can count on me to express myself.
Be transparent, be adaptable.
Be tasteful and tasteless, to be clear.
Have dinner with business owners.
Be esteemed by NASA employees.

Be 20mins late to the family cookout,
stumbling in, carrying plastic cutlery
and a 32 pack of Deer Park.
Adding my two cents to the hip hop dialogue
and the music history "back in my day" debates.

But this isn't a poem about cultural appropriation, or the proper way to ask
someone to pass the bread.

You can count on me to be refreshing.
To produce an idea that'll change the trajectory
of a head scratching project.
To be the life of the party when the ingredients is right.
To be present, cool and content
when the ingredients is right.

To bring and be balance.

But this isn't a poem about me and my ability to walk social balance beams blind folded.

This may be a poem about control.
This may be a poem about self security and awareness.

Humility.

But this can't be a poem about humility
because once you think you've got it you've already lost it.
But this may be a poem about not loosing yourself.

This may be a poem about not just keeping your cool
but keeping yourself cool.
When the heat of life has February's farewell
feeling like July if June gave it the flu.

This may be a poem about your social life
keeping you on your toes.
When the best way to deal with the unexpected
is to not expect anything.
When the best way to deal with the unknown
is to never feel like you know it all.

This may be a poem about how we should all take a page out of water's book.

How to belong everywhere you're poured.
How to be free.
Formless, shapeless, careless, even.
Essential and dangerous at the same time.

AUTHOR'S NOTES:

On Earth, As It Is In Water cover photo was taken by Gillian Dwyer in Australia 2021.

"Ubiquity" is a compete ode to the classic Roy Ayers & Ubiquity song "Everybody Loves The Sunshine."

"Irish Goodbye" is inspired by the song "Ketchum, ID" by Boy Genius.

"The Race Thing" is the complete poetic lyrics of the theme song written and composed by Jordon Stanley, Shea Springer, and Kentavius Jones for The Race Thing podcast.

"Take Me There" is inspired by a piece of art titled "The Still" by Gillian Dwyer. A charcoal piece of a train at the station.

"5/26/21" was written during the thunderstorm that followed the Blue Angles air show in Annapolis MD, May 2021.

"Four Wishes For You" was inspired and dedicated to Heather Cate.

"Subscribing To Resilience" is inspired by Javier Santiago's song Subscribing To Resilience on his B Sides: The Phoenix Sessions album.

ABOUT THE AUTHOR

JORDON L. STANLEY is a poet and musician from Maryland. He studied Music Education at the University of Maryland, Eastern Shore and has been a music educator for 9 years. His album "Creative Sessions Vol. 1" released in 2021, following his first poetry collection *Poems From A Poem* in 2019. You can find his website at www.jordonlstanley.com.